I keep my body clean.

Me mantengo limpio.

Wearing clean clothes feels great.

Me siento muy bien cuando me pongo ropa limpia.

I brush my hair every morning.

Me peino todas las mañanas.

I gently clean my ears.

Me limpio los oídos con mucho cuidado.

My teeth need brushing every day.

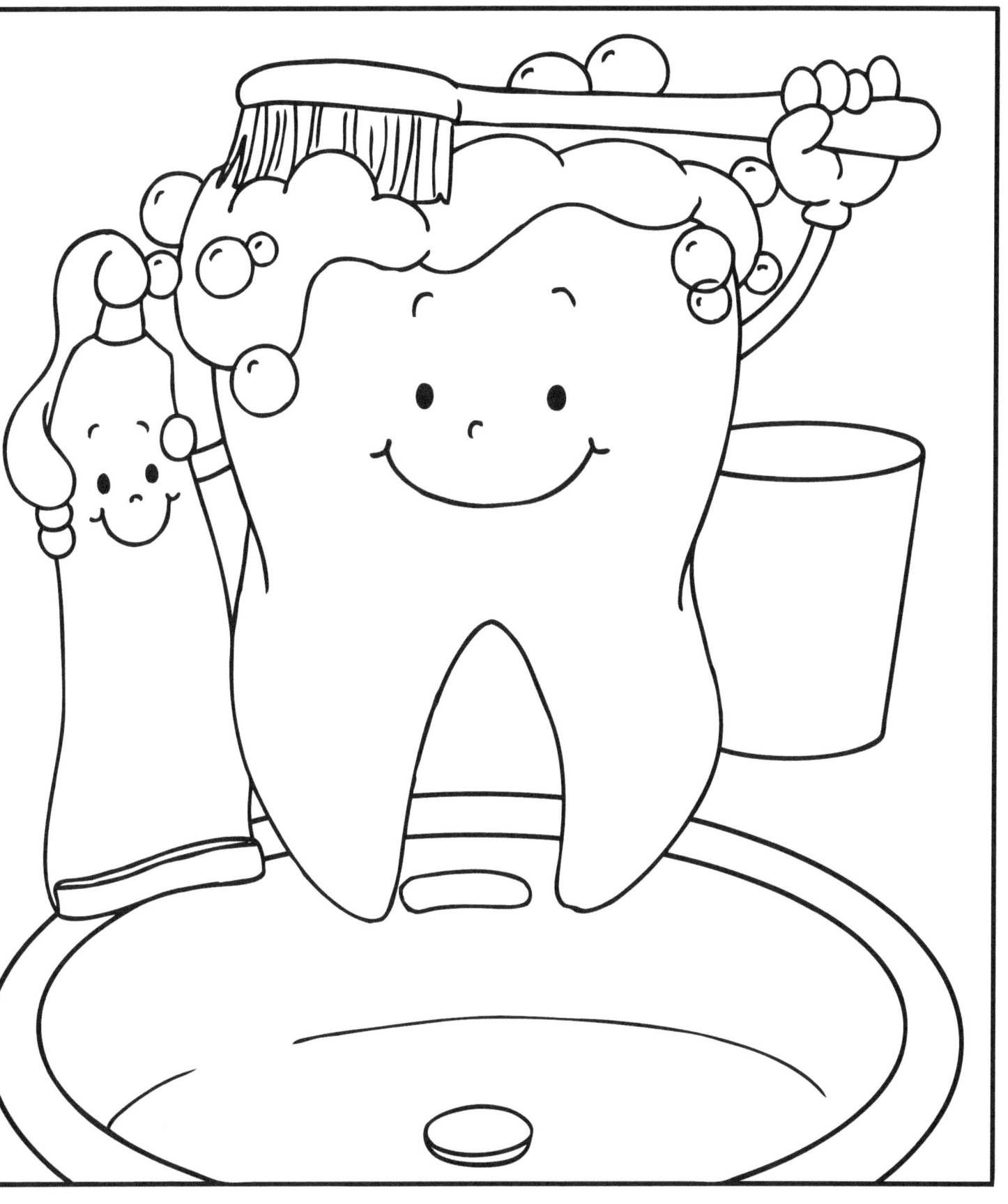

Debo cepillarme los dientes todos los días.

The dentist checks my teeth.

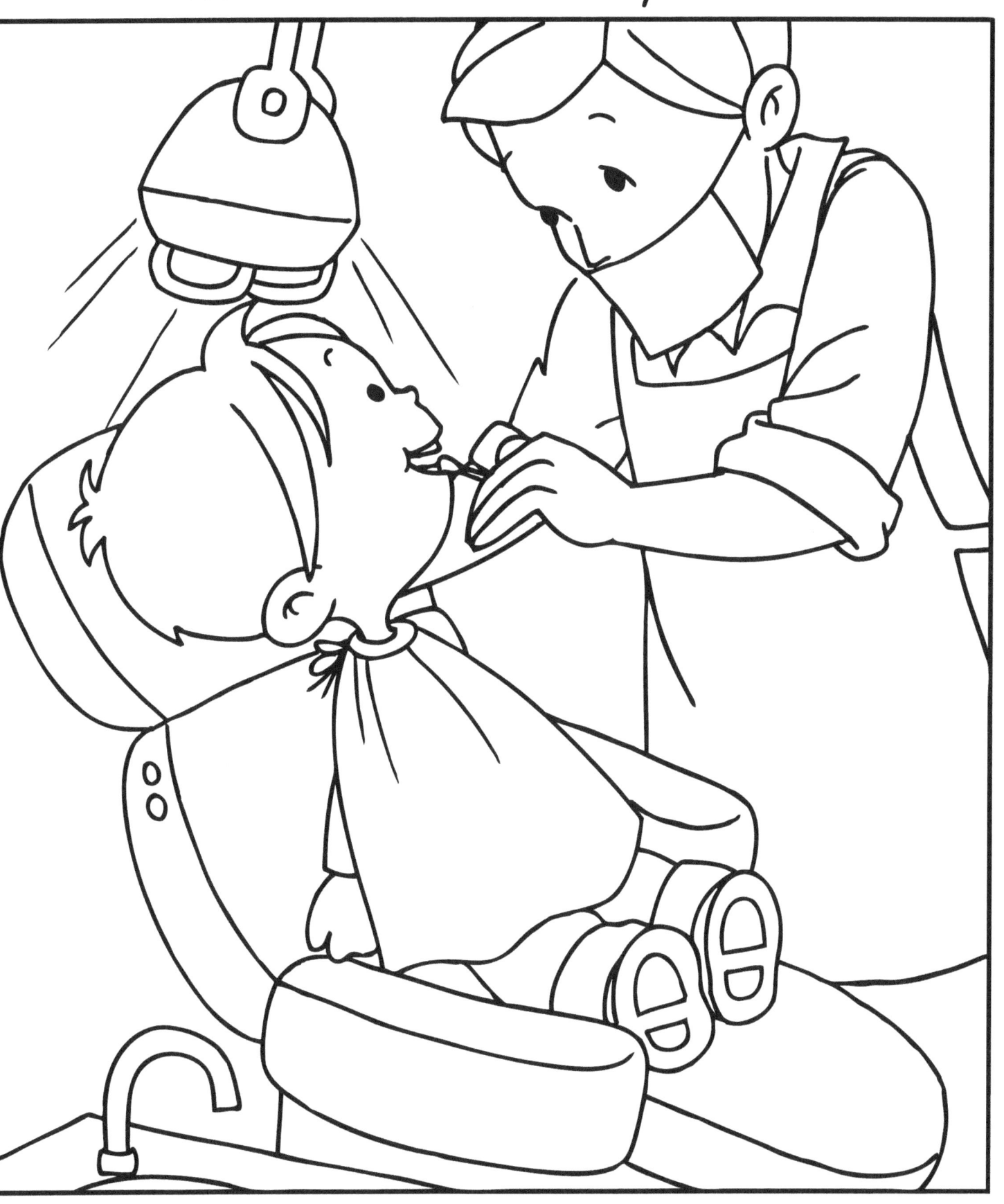

El dentista me revisa los dientes.

Fresh air and sunshine are good for me.

El aire fresco y el sol me hacen bien.

My body needs exercise.

Mi cuerpo necesita ejercicio.

I watch out for the sun.

Me cuido del sol.

Reading in good light is important.

Es importante leer con buena luz.

I have good posture.

Mantengo una buena postura.

Each morning I make my bed.

Tiendo mi cama todos los días.

I put away my toys after play.

Cuando termino de jugar, guardo mis juguetes.

I think happy thoughts.

Pienso en cosas positivas.

I eat with good manners.

Como con buenos modales.

Good foods make my body happy.

La comida sana me hace bien.

My body needs lots of water.

Mi cuerpo necesita mucha agua.

I get plenty of rest.

Descanso todo lo necesario.

I wash my hands often.

Me lavo las manos con frecuencia.

I take good care of things.

Cuido muy bien las cosas.

I wear a seat belt in the car.

Uso el cinturón de seguridad.

It's important to play safely.

Conviene ser cuidadosos al jugar.

I need to be kind and polite.

Tengo que ser amable y educado.

My face wears a big smile.

Siempre luzco una gran sonrisa.

I enjoy my food.

Saboreo lo que como.

I eat healthy snacks.

Me alimento sanamente.

I finish all my food.

Me termino toda la comida.

I drink lots of water.

Bebo mucha agua.

Too much candy isn't good for my body.

Comer demasiados dulces me hace daño.

I only eat sweets on special occasions.

Solo como dulces en ocasiones especiales.

I eat lots of vegetables.

Como muchas verduras.

I pick a fruit over cookies.

Elijo una fruta en lugar de galletas.

I don't eat many processed foods.

No como muchos alimentos procesados.

Fresh foods are best for me.

Es mejor comer alimentos frescos.

I like foods that are not too greasy.

Prefiero alimentos con poca grasa.

Natural sugars are the best.

Los azúcares naturales son los mejores.

I shouldn't eat too fast.

No debería comer demasiado rápido.

I should take it easy right after eating.

Después de comer me tomo las cosas con calma.

Eating only a little before bed helps me sleep better.

Comer poco antes de irme a la cama
me ayuda a dormir mejor.

Soft drinks are not good for me.

No es saludable beber refrescos.

I eat from all the food groups.

Como de todos los grupos de alimentos.

Grains and breads

Granos y cereales

Vegetables

Verduras

Fruit

Frutas

Meat and fish

Carne y pescado

Beans and nuts

Legumbres y semillas

Eggs and milk

Huevos y lácteos

Sweets are for special occasions.

Los dulces son para ocasiones especiales.

www.kidible.eu

Published by iCharacter Ltd. (Ireland)
Kidible is an imprint of iCharacter Ltd.
By Agnes de Bezenac

Copyright © 2014 by iCharacter Limited. All rights reserved. No part of this book may be reproduced in any form or by any electronic or mechanical means, including information storage and retrieval systems, without written permission from the publisher or author, except in the case of a reviewer, who may quote brief passages embodied in critical articles or in a review.

www.ingramcontent.com/pod-product-compliance
Lightning Source LLC
Chambersburg PA
CBHW080026080526
44586CB00017B/2143